KV-325-444

CREATE YOUR OWN
NATURE
RESERVE
JANET KELLY

SIMON & SCHUSTER
LONDON • SYDNEY • NEW YORK • TOKYO • SINGAPORE • TORONTO

For my mother P.K.

First published in 1991
by Simon & Schuster Young Books

Simon & Schuster Young Books
Wolsey House, Wolsey Road,
Hemel Hempstead, Herts HP2 4SS.

Text © 1991 Janet Kelly
Illustrations © 1991 Simon & Schuster Young Books

Design: David West
Children's Book Design
Editor: Ros Mair
Illustrator: Neil Bulpitt

Printed and bound in Belgium
by Proost International Book Production

A CIP catalogue record for this book is available
from the British Library.

ISBN 0 7500 0841 5

Some of the activities will require the help of
an adult.

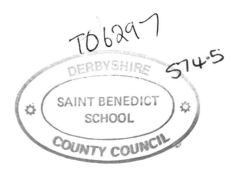

CONTENTS

WHY CREATE A NATURE RESERVE?

In the last 50 years large areas of countryside have been destroyed. Ponds, marshes, woodlands and meadows have gone to make way for factories, houses and roads. Farmers have used chemicals to kill weeds in their crops. Make a few changes to your garden, and soon you will have your own nature reserve to study and enjoy.

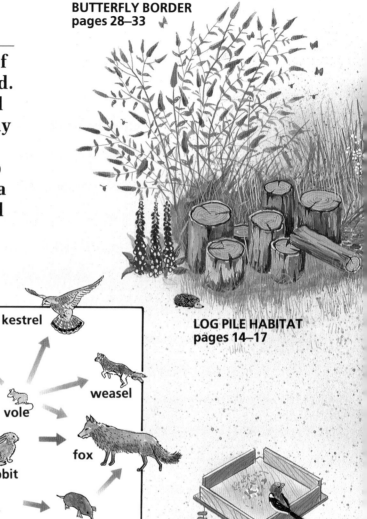

BUTTERFLY BORDER
pages 28–33

LOG PILE HABITAT
pages 14–17

HELPING ANIMALS
pages 34–39

FOOD WEB

blue tit

hedgehog

owl

kestrel

weasel

slug

vole

fox

caterpillar

sun

grass

rabbit

light energy

earthworm

mole

FOOD CHAIN

grass → rabbit (herbivore) → fox (carnivore)

The place where an animal or plant lives is called its habitat. Each habitat contains many different types (species) of animal and plant. All of them need energy to survive. Green plants trap light energy from the sun and use it to make food. Animals eat plants (herbivores) or animals (carnivores) to obtain energy.

6

MEADOW HABITAT
pages 24–27

WOODLAND HABITAT
pages 8–13

WETLAND HABITAT
pages 18–23

PATIO GARDENS
pages 40–41

WHAT DO HABITATS PROVIDE?

They must provide animals with food, protection from predators and bad weather, and a place to have their young.

food

protection from predators

nectar

place to have young

berries

shelter

MAKING A WOODLAND HABITAT

The natural vegetation of much of the British Isles is deciduous woodland, with oak, birch, ash and beech trees, but in the last 45 years over half of it has been destroyed and its wildlife lost. Many trees have been planted but many are not native, like the horse chestnut, and they support little wildlife. About 6,500 kilometres of hedgerows are being uprooted a year.

STRUCTURE OF A WOOD

Natural woodlands have four layers of vegetation:
The canopy consists of trees such as oak, beech, lime and scots pine.
Shrubs include hazel, elder and holly.
Herbs include bluebells, primroses, snowdrops, violets, grasses and ferns.
The ground itself is covered with mosses and fungi.

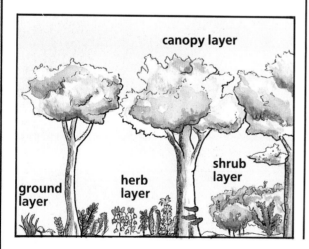

canopy layer

shrub layer

herb layer

ground layer

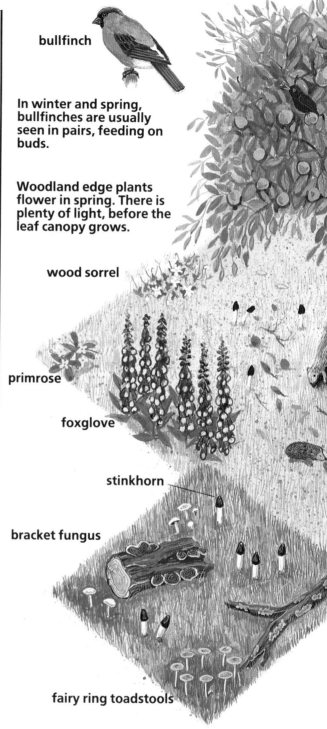

bullfinch

In winter and spring, bullfinches are usually seen in pairs, feeding on buds.

Woodland edge plants flower in spring. There is plenty of light, before the leaf canopy grows.

wood sorrel

primrose

foxglove

stinkhorn

bracket fungus

fairy ring toadstools

Fungi cannot make their own food in the way other plants can. Many get their energy by living on and breaking down dead material such as fallen trees, logs and dead leaves.

In spring, queen wasps feed on nectar before building paper nests made from saliva and wood scraped from dead trees. In autumn, worker wasps eat ripe apples.

wasp

bluebells

dunnock (hedge sparrow)

Shrubs provide nest sites for dunnocks, blackbirds and song thrushes. Great and blue tits nest in holes in trees.

longhorn beetle

bark beetle

cockchafer

Longhorn and bark beetles scurry along the bark, and cockchafers (maybugs) feed on young shoots.

PLANTING YOUR WOODLAND EDGE

The smallest garden may have room for one tree, and by planting shrubs beneath it, with wildflowers and a log pile, you will have a woodland edge rich in wildlife.

WHAT YOU NEED:

flowers

watering can

shrub

fork

spade

stake

leaf mould

tie

tree

PLANTING YOUR TREE

When to plant: October to March.
Where to plant: Bottom or side of the garden, not near the house.
How to plant:
1 Water the roots of your tree. Dig a large hole, loosen the soil at the bottom.
2 Add leaf mould and drive in a stake.
3 Hold the tree upright, add soil, attach ties, and water.

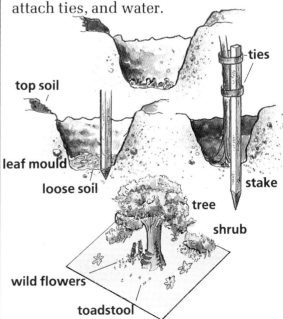

top soil

leaf mould

loose soil

ties

stake

tree

shrub

wild flowers

toadstool

LOOKING AFTER YOUR TREE

In the first summer after planting and in dry weather, water the tree regularly. Bin liners, or chopped bark round its base keeps moisture in and weeds down. Loosen the ties as the tree grows.

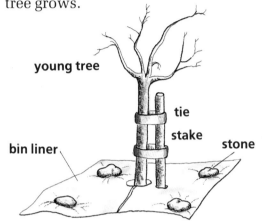

young tree

tie

stake

bin liner

stone

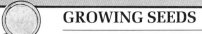

GROWING SEEDS

Collect ripe fruits in September eg. acorns or maple. Soak them in water overnight to soften them, then plant them in a pot of sandy soil. Put them outside for winter. You will see the seedlings in spring.

GROWING A TREE FROM SEED:

1 Plant in damp soil.   **2** Keep soil moist.

INSECTS AND FLOWERS

Bees and wasps are attracted to flowers by their colour and scent. When collecting nectar, pollen from the male stamens sticks to their legs and hairy bodies. If they visit another flower of the same type, pollen rubs onto the female stigma. This is pollination. Fertilization follows and the ovules become seeds that can grow into new plants. Honey bees also collect pollen to feed to their larvae.

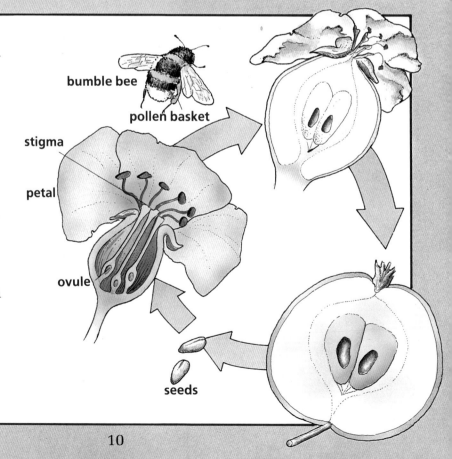

bumble bee

pollen basket

stigma

petal

ovule

seeds

Acorns and hazelnuts can be trodden into the ground with your foot wherever you would like them to grow, but beware, the local squirrel or jay may find them first!

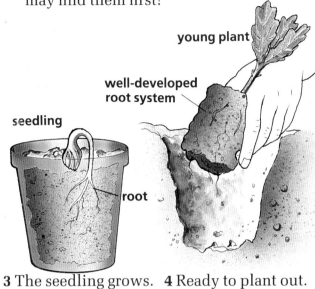

young plant

well-developed root system

seedling

root

3 The seedling grows.   **4** Ready to plant out.

TREES FOR YOUR RESERVE

Plant native trees that support the greatest variety of wildlife. The numbers show how many species of insects that type of tree can support.

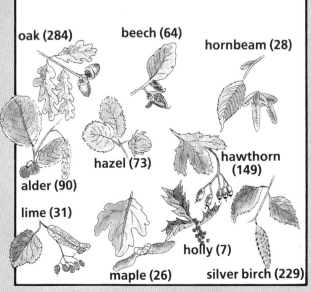

oak (284)   beech (64)

hornbeam (28)

hazel (73)   hawthorn (149)

alder (90)

lime (31)

holly (7)

maple (26)   silver birch (229)

HAVE YOU SPOTTED?

Birds will be frequent visitors to your woodland edge (see below and page 37). On warm, still evenings try "sugaring" tree trunks to attract insects (see page 30). Later examine your catch by torchlight.

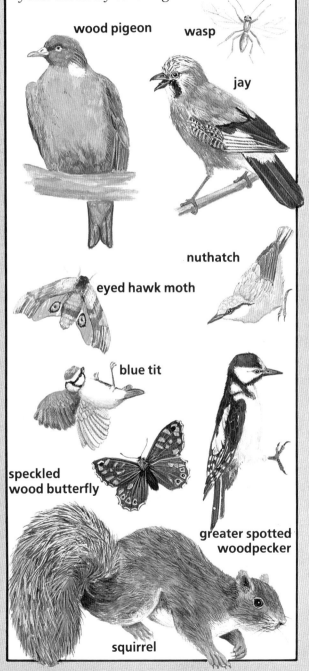

wood pigeon   wasp

jay

nuthatch

eyed hawk moth

blue tit

speckled wood butterfly

greater spotted woodpecker

squirrel

FINDING WOODLAND ANIMALS

You can collect insects and other small animals from trees and shrubs using an upturned light coloured umbrella as shown, or a white sheet spread out on the ground. Tap the branch with a stick and the animals will fall onto the sheet or umbrella and can be examined, identified and then released.

use umbrella to catch insects

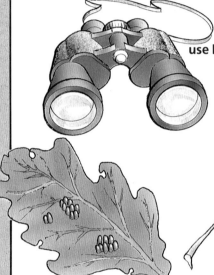

use binoculars for spotting birds

use a magnifying glass to look for insects

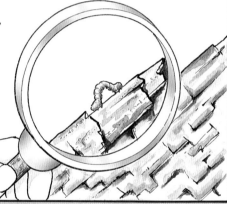

look under leaves for caterpillars and eggs

DID YOU KNOW?

In autumn jays collect vast numbers of acorns, taking them in the beak and throat pouch to fields to bury them. In winter they return to eat them – those they miss may grow into oak trees.

Squirrels do not hibernate in winter. They usually look for food every day. If it is very cold and wet, they may stay in their dreys for one or two days.

BE A CONSERVATIONIST NOT A COLLECTOR

Protect flowers. **NEVER** dig up a wildflower from the countryside. Avoid picking flowers as this prevents them producing seeds. It is against the law to pick rare flowers.

Bird's nests and eggs. It is against the law to disturb nesting birds. **NEVER** collect their eggs. Hedgerow birds build new nests each year; in autumn, find an old nest and see what it is made of.

A HEDGEROW HABITAT

A hedge can add much to your nature reserve. Plant hawthorn about every metre, with field maple, dog rose, guelder rose, holly and wild privet. You don't need stakes. Hedgerow plants and many woodland plants will grow along the bottom. If the soil is chalky, plant cowslips.

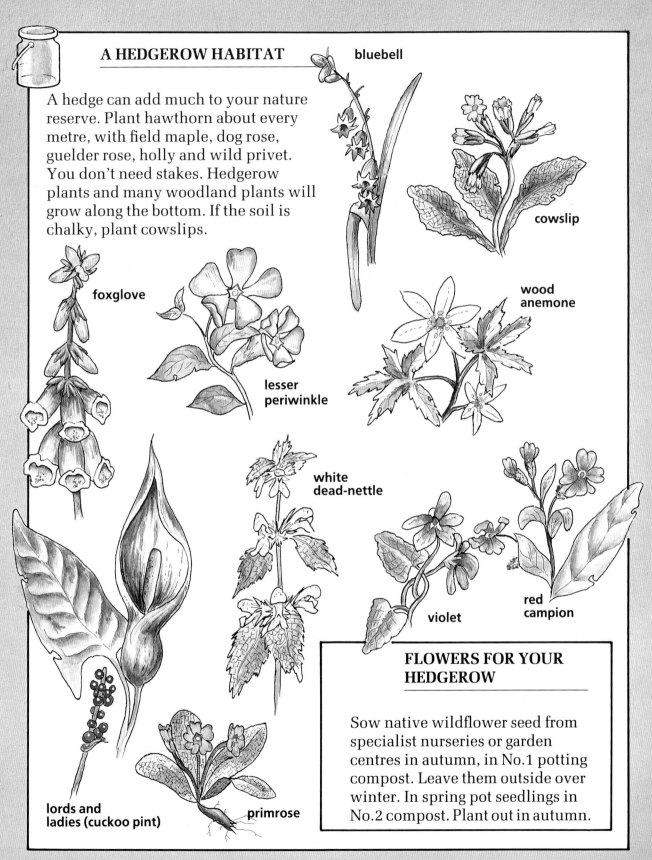

bluebell

cowslip

foxglove

lesser periwinkle

wood anemone

white dead-nettle

violet

red campion

lords and ladies (cuckoo pint)

primrose

FLOWERS FOR YOUR HEDGEROW

Sow native wildflower seed from specialist nurseries or garden centres in autumn, in No.1 potting compost. Leave them outside over winter. In spring pot seedlings in No.2 compost. Plant out in autumn.

MAKING A LOG PILE HABITAT

The smallest backyard can find room for a log pile. Once set up you will be amazed how quickly the wildlife moves in. Make it more exciting by adding dead leaves, twigs, chopped bark and empty flower pots; a bundle of hollow canes pushed between the logs may attract nesting bees. Try and get recently felled logs from different types of tree; old logs are not such a good source of food.

DECOMPOSITION AND RECYCLING

Bacteria, fungi, earthworms, millipedes and woodlice feed on dead wood and leaves and break them down into simple chemicals (**1**). This is known as decomposition. The chemicals are released into the soil (**2**) and taken up again by plant roots (**3**); they have been recycled. When the plant dies the process begins again (**4**). Carbon dioxide is released into the air (**5**).

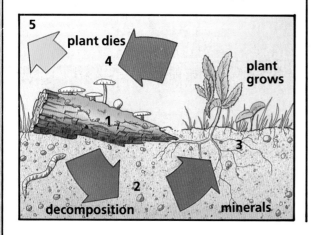

5 plant dies
4
plant grows
1
3
2
decomposition
minerals

spiders make webs between the logs to catch prey

thrushes and blackbirds find food under the leaves and chopped bark

wrens look for spiders to eat

fungi grow

snails and slugs hibernate and hide from predators under logs and flower pots

voles build nests amongst logs

14

woodlice and millipedes find food under the moist bark

robins shelter and nest in piles of twigs

hedgehogs hibernate in piles of dead leaves

toads and newts shelter under moist logs

LOG PILE MATERIALS

WHAT YOU NEED:

chopped bark

slices of tree trunk or bricks

clay flower pots

dead leaves

lengths of tree trunk (2+ metres)

twigs

canes

Where to put it Choose a site at the bottom of the garden, alongside a fence or wall, under a tree, or at the edge of your woodland area.

How to make it
1 Spread the bark over the ground where your log pile is going to be.
2 Stack the logs loosely on top with taller logs at the back.
3 Place the flower pots upside down or on their sides amongst the logs.
4 Make a pile of twigs and a heap of leaf litter alongside the logs.
5 Wait for the animals to move in!

tall logs at back

twigs

dead leaves

flower pots

chopped bark from garden centre

15

FINDING ANIMALS

LOOKING UNDER LOGS

1 Lift edge and collect animal with some soil on a plastic spoon.

2 Put animals into a prepared container.
3 Replace log carefully in its original position.

LOOKING UNDER BARK

1 Lift up a small section of bark with a screwdriver.
2 Remove any animals with a damp paintbrush.
3 Transfer the animals to a prepared container. Only remove a small section of bark.

LOOKING UNDER LOGS:

1

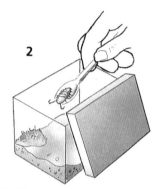
2

3

LOOKING UNDER BARK:

1

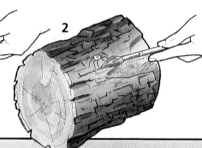
2

3

HAVE YOU SPOTTED?

These are a few of the animals that may be living in your log pile.

centipede

spider

earthworm

millipede

slug

harvestman

beetle larva (grub)

woodlouse

snail

ground beetle

earwig

PITFALL TRAPS

Set them next to your log pile. Bait them with dog or cat food to attract carnivores such as ground beetles. Leave them overnight. Next day empty them, identify, count and release the animals. Compare results from daytime catches and try different baits.

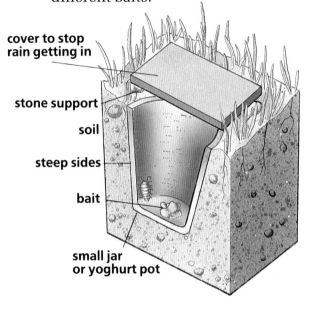

cover to stop rain getting in

stone support

soil

steep sides

bait

small jar or yoghurt pot

DID YOU KNOW?

The woodlouse has about 65 common names, like tiggy hog, sink louse, bibble bug, slater, cudworm, sow bug and coffin cutter. One type which can roll up into a ball is the "pill bug"; in the past it was thought to cure headaches, stomach problems and the disease, tuberculosis.

In the time of Queen Elizabeth I, spiders webs were put on wounds to stop them bleeding.

INVESTIGATING WOODLICE

You may have found large numbers of woodlice under the bark and logs, but why are they there? Is it because it is dark or damp or because there is food? Let's investigate.

What to do Set up a tank as shown below, placing an equal number of wet and dry leaves on each side. Put 10–20 woodlice in the centre of the tank, replace the lid and put it in the dark. Next day examine the leaf piles and count how many woodlice are in each.

What you discover You will probably find more woodlice in the damp leaves. This is because the "skin", or cuticle, of a woodlouse is not waterproof. In dry conditions they lose water and die.

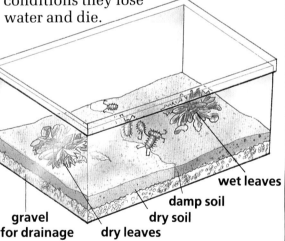

wet leaves

damp soil

dry soil

gravel for drainage

dry leaves

BE A CONSERVATIONIST NOT A COLLECTOR

Look closely at woodlice, snails, slugs and millipedes. Keep them in a tank with gravel, damp soil, moss, bark and leaf litter. After 2 weeks, always release them.

MAKING A WETLAND HABITAT

In the last 100 years many wetland habitats have been lost. Marshland has been drained, ponds and ditches filled in, and rivers and streams have been polluted by chemicals. This has meant a great loss of wildlife, and in some areas even the common frog is rare. The future of many plants and animals may lie in the network of garden ponds spread across the country.

LIFE CYCLES OF INSECTS

There are two types of life cycle. Young stages of mayflies are called nymphs. They look like adults but lack wings. Young stages of butterflies are called larvae. They change into pupae and then adults (see page 32). Below is the life cycle of the mayfly.

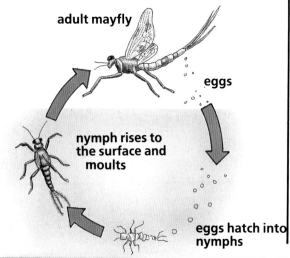

adult mayfly

eggs

nymph rises to the surface and moults

eggs hatch into nymphs

In summer swallows swoop low over the water collecting insects in their wide mouths.

swallow

mayfly

Adult mayflies live for 1–2 days and then die; they do not feed.

Gently sloping sides or ramp stop hedgehogs drowning.

hedgehog

frog

great diving beetle

water boatman

Frogs, toads and newts hibernate in winter. In spring they return to ponds to breed.

toad

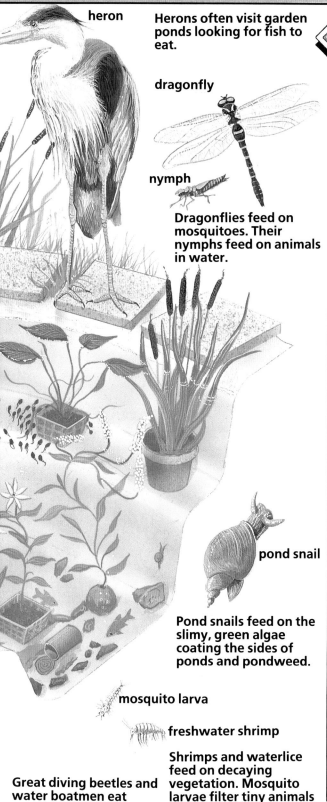

heron Herons often visit garden ponds looking for fish to eat.

dragonfly

nymph

Dragonflies feed on mosquitoes. Their nymphs feed on animals in water.

pond snail

Pond snails feed on the slimy, green algae coating the sides of ponds and pondweed.

mosquito larva

freshwater shrimp

Shrimps and waterlice feed on decaying vegetation. Mosquito larvae filter tiny animals and plants.

Great diving beetles and water boatmen eat worms, insects, tadpoles.

MAKING YOUR POND

WHAT YOU NEED:

butyl liner or sheet of polythene

paving stones

stones

drain pipe

old carpet

sand

pond plants

When to build April or May.
Where to plant Open flat ground, with no overhanging trees.
How to make it Make a plan and mark the area. Dig a hole with gently sloping sides 60 cm at its deepest. Line with a thick layer of sand or carpet. Hold the liner down with stones and slowly fill with water.

fill pond from hosepipe

liner

pipes for animals to hide in

stones for animals to colonize

19

HOW TO PLANT YOUR WETLAND

Plant in April or May with marsh and aquatic plants.

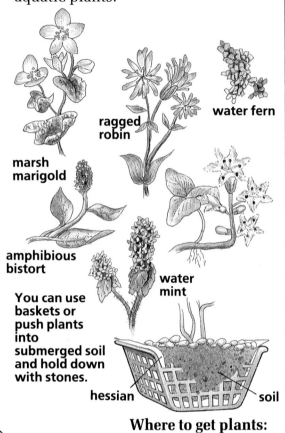

ragged robin

water fern

marsh marigold

amphibious bistort

water mint

You can use baskets or push plants into submerged soil and hold down with stones.

hessian

soil

Where to get plants: NEVER from local ponds. Ask friends if they have any to spare.

For plants in deep water tie the plant and soil in a hessian bag and toss it in.

PLANTS FOR YOUR POND

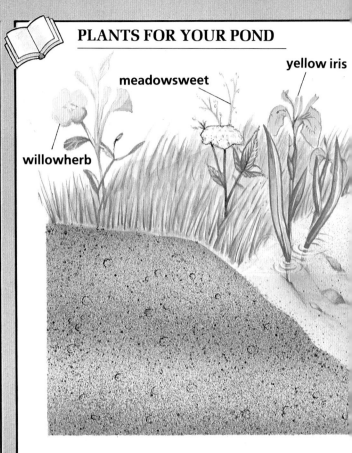

meadowsweet

yellow iris

willowherb

INTRODUCING POND ANIMALS

You will be surprised how quickly wildlife appears. Some animals fly in, others come in with pondweed or are brought by birds drinking at the water's edge.

dragonfly (flies in)

blackbird may bring eggs and seeds on its feet or in its beak.

snail's eggs on water plant

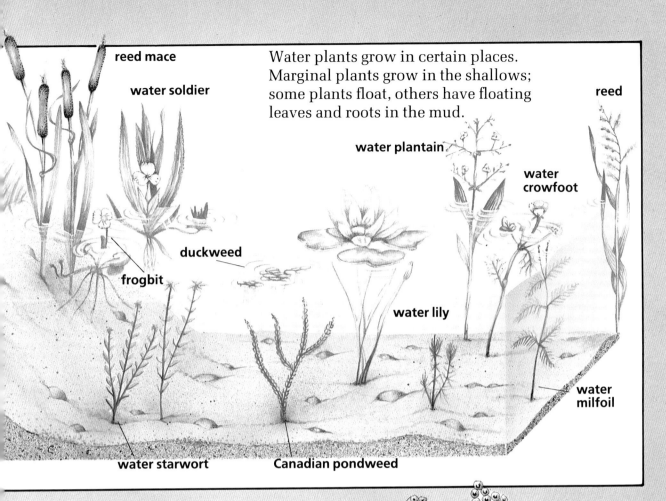

reed mace

water soldier

Water plants grow in certain places. Marginal plants grow in the shallows; some plants float, others have floating leaves and roots in the mud.

reed

water plantain

water crowfoot

duckweed

frogbit

water lily

water milfoil

water starwort

Canadian pondweed

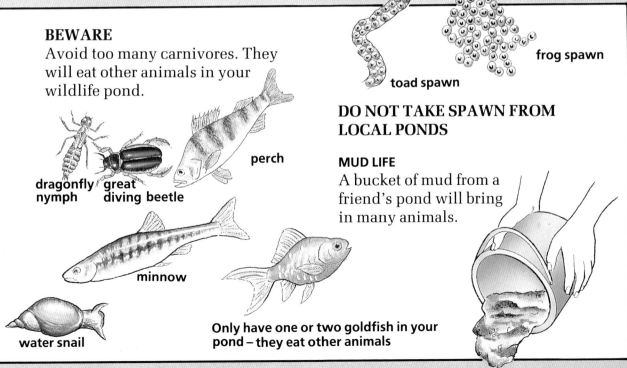

BEWARE

Avoid too many carnivores. They will eat other animals in your wildlife pond.

frog spawn

toad spawn

DO NOT TAKE SPAWN FROM LOCAL PONDS

perch

MUD LIFE

A bucket of mud from a friend's pond will bring in many animals.

dragonfly nymph

great diving beetle

minnow

water snail

Only have one or two goldfish in your pond – they eat other animals

LOOKING AT POND WATER

Collect pond animals with a plastic kitchen sieve or net. Move this gently through the water, then put the catch in a container with some water. Don't handle the animals; use a pipette, paintbrush or plastic spoon. When identified put them back in the pond.

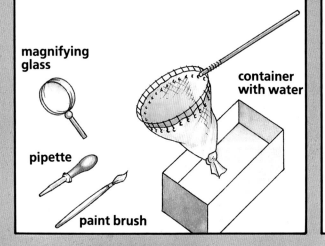

magnifying glass

container with water

pipette

paint brush

CATCHING LEECHES

If you find leeches in your pond don't worry, the species that sucks human blood is very rare. Some suck the blood of waterbirds, frogs and fish; others swallow prey, such as tadpoles, whole. They often lurk in waterweed but you can set a trap for them by lowering a jam jar, with raw meat in it, into the pond on a piece of string, or by tossing in a piece of raw meat on a string. Next day haul in the bait and see what you've got.

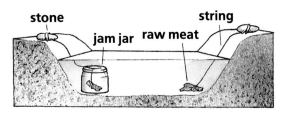

stone

string

jam jar   raw meat

LOOKING AT TADPOLES

Life cycle of a frog

Metamorphosis occurs when tadpoles change into frogs. Transfer a little frogspawn into a tank containing pond water and weed. Add fresh pond water occasionally. Before 8 weeks tadpoles feed on plants, but then they become carnivores. Hang raw meat on a string over the side of the tank and change it daily. When their tails begin to shorten, put them back in the pond.

egg

tadpole in jelly

1

2

6

3

newly hatched tadpole

tail absorbed, froglet leaves water

4

5

front legs emerge

hind legs develop at 6/7 weeks

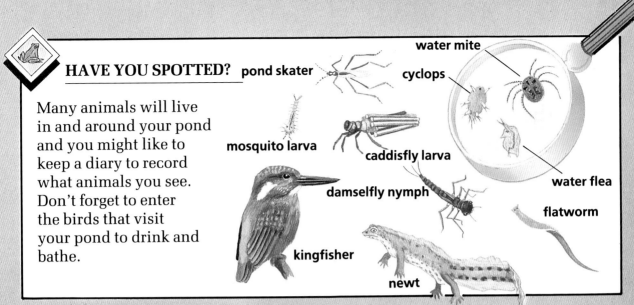

HAVE YOU SPOTTED?

Many animals will live in and around your pond and you might like to keep a diary to record what animals you see. Don't forget to enter the birds that visit your pond to drink and bathe.

pond skater

water mite

cyclops

mosquito larva

caddisfly larva

damselfly nymph

water flea

flatworm

kingfisher

newt

MAKING AN AQUARIUM

For a freshwater aquarium collect water plants, snails, freshwater lice and shrimps and caddis larvae. Avoid carnivores such as dragonfly nymphs. Put the tank in the shade; feed the animals by occasionally adding live daphnia from your pond or a pet shop.

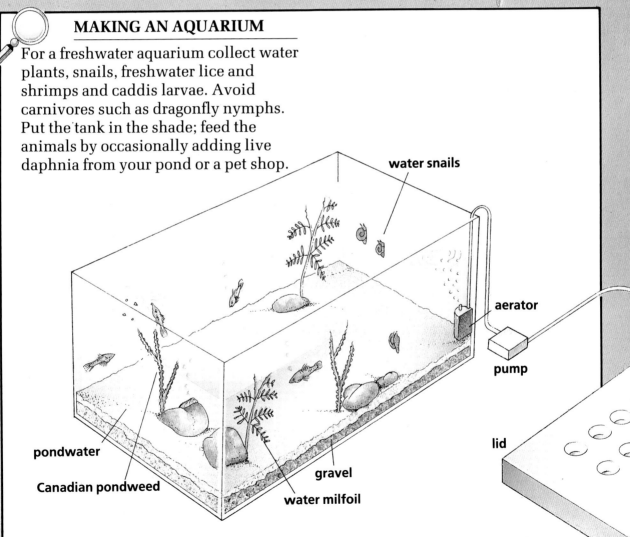

water snails

aerator

pump

lid

pondwater

Canadian pondweed

gravel

water milfoil

MAKING A MEADOW

Unspoilt meadows contain many different types of grasses and wildflowers, but today they are very rare. In the last 50 years, 96 per cent of old pasture has gone. Some wildflowers are lost forever, and animals like skylarks are less common. Many farmers have replaced old hay meadows with a few grasses that support less wildlife.

THE HAY MEADOW YEAR

In the past a yearly pattern of mowing and grazing provided ideal conditions for certain wildflowers. Sheep and cattle grazed on the meadows during winter; they left in spring to allow the plants to grow, flower and seed. In June the hay was cut, left to dry and shed seed and then collected. In autumn the cattle returned and trod the seeds into the ground.

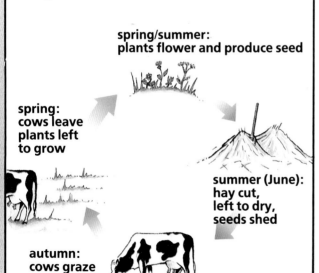

spring/summer:
plants flower and produce seed

spring:
cows leave
plants left
to grow

summer (June):
hay cut,
left to dry,
seeds shed

autumn:
cows graze

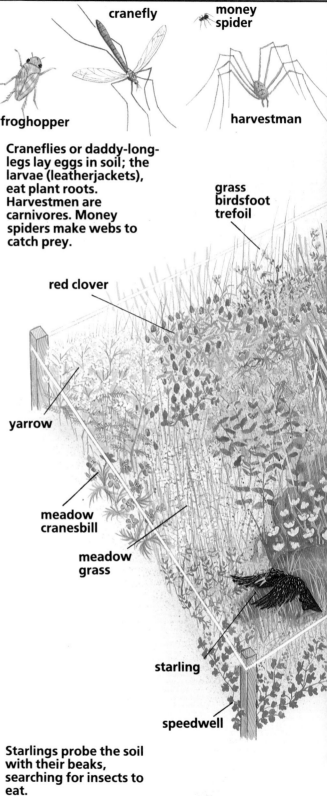

cranefly

money
spider

froghopper

harvestman

Craneflies or daddy-long-legs lay eggs in soil; the larvae (leatherjackets), eat plant roots. Harvestmen are carnivores. Money spiders make webs to catch prey.

grass
birdsfoot
trefoil

red clover

yarrow

meadow
cranesbill

meadow
grass

starling

speedwell

Starlings probe the soil with their beaks, searching for insects to eat.

six-spot burnet moth

meadow foxtail

meadow brown butterfly and caterpillar

The six-spot burnet moth is active during the day, unlike most moths. Meadow brown butterflies fly slowly over the meadow. Its caterpillars feed on grasses.

knapweed

timothy grass

scabious

molehill

ox-eye daisy

meadow buttercup

mole

shrew

Moles search for earthworms to eat, along their tunnels.

Voles and shrews hide from predators in the meadow. Voles feed on grasses; shrews eat insects, worms and slugs.

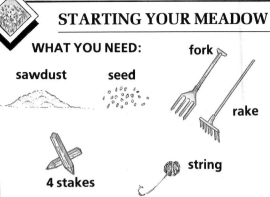

STARTING YOUR MEADOW

WHAT YOU NEED:

sawdust   seed   fork

4 stakes   rake   string

When to sow: September is best.
What to sow: Native wildflower mix, 2 or 3 grass species (not rye grass).
How to make it: Poor soil is best; dig it over, remove stones and rake until it is fine. Sow the grass, then the wildflower seed, and firm the soil. Grasses will grow in autumn, wildflowers the next spring.

MEADOWS FROM LAWNS

This is easy if you have a lawn with lots of weeds. Simply mark out an area and stop mowing it. Plan your mowing (see page 26) and have a spring or summer flowering meadow.

SUCCESS WITH YOUR MEADOW

If you want a meadow with lots of different wildflowers, you must have "poor" soil, so:

never add fertilizer to your meadow; and

always remove the clippings with a rake. If clippings are left they will rot down, or decompose, and this releases chemicals which will make the soil more fertile.

YOUR SPRING MEADOW

In the first spring count how many different types of wildflowers you can find in your new meadow. If it doesn't have many you can try adding more.

In autumn rip through your meadow with a rake to make bare patches, then sow wildflower seed on them. Buy potted wildflowers from nurseries or put your new seedlings in pots (see page 13) and plant them later.

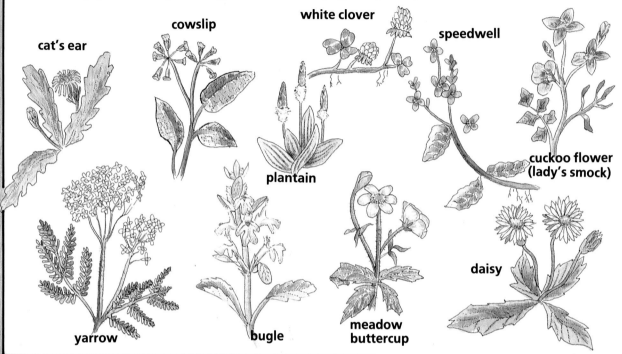

cat's ear

cowslip

white clover

speedwell

plantain

cuckoo flower (lady's smock)

yarrow

bugle

meadow buttercup

daisy

MOWING YOUR MEADOW

Mow spring flowering meadows in June when the flowers have died. Leave the clippings for a week to let the seeds fall onto the soil, then rake. Mow regularly until autumn. Mow summer flowering meadows until June, then leave to flower. Mow again and rake in autumn.

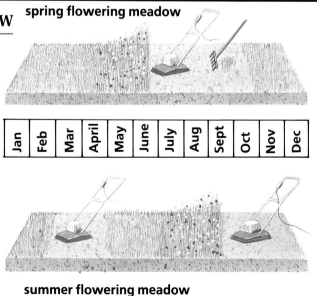

spring flowering meadow

Jan	Feb	Mar	April	May	June	July	Aug	Sept	Oct	Nov	Dec

summer flowering meadow

A CORNFIELD PATCH

You could turn any small piece of ground into a cornfield patch. In September sow a mixture of cornfield seeds (see page 13); leave to flower the next summer. In autumn dig the plants out, but let the seeds be shed.

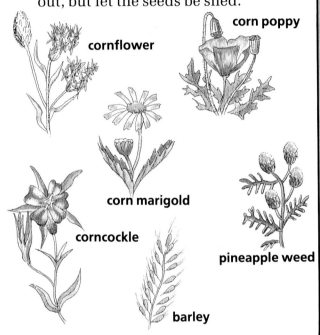

corn poppy

cornflower

corn marigold

corncockle

pineapple weed

barley

FINDING ANIMALS

You can make a sweep net from an old tennis racquet frame and a long bag made from a white sheet. Sweep the net through the grass.

HAVE YOU SPOTTED?

Here are some more animals you may see in your meadow:

goldfinch (feeds on seed heads)

wolf spider

cardinal beetle

slow worm

aphid (greenfly)

cricket

grass snake

capsid bug

rabbit

seven-spot ladybird

shield bug

short-tailed vole

BE A CONSERVATIONIST NOT A COLLECTOR

Collect wildflower seed from the garden or roadside verges. **NEVER** collect seeds of rare plants, only take seeds where there are lots of plants. Sow as soon as possible.

MAKING A BUTTERFLY BORDER

In recent years the numbers of butterflies have gone down drastically. Loss of woodland, hedgerows, grassland and meadowland habitats has been partly to blame as this has meant fewer wildflowers on which butterflies feed. Your nature reserve can play its part in helping them. You can grow plants which will encourage butterflies, moths, bees and other insects to visit and breed.

WHY INSECTS VISIT GARDENS

Butterflies and other insects will fly into your nature reserve in search of nectar to feed on, but if you want them to breed you must provide the right food plant for the caterpillars. First you need to find out which butterfly visitors you have. In autumn small tortoiseshell and brimstone butterflies may come into your reserve to hibernate.

garden tiger moth

magpie moth

large skipper

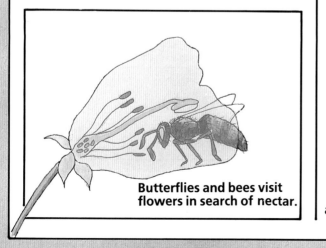

Butterflies and bees visit flowers in search of nectar.

All butterflies and moths, honey bees, bumble bees, hoverflies (including the drone fly) and ants feed on nectar too.

drone fly

ant

hover fly

bee fly

28

peacock

small tortoiseshell

small heath

Caterpillars eat leaves. If you grow a selection of their food plants you can encourage butterflies and moths to breed in your reserve.

honey bee

bumble bee

GROWING PLANTS

From seed In spring, sow Californian poppy, and candytuft in gaps in the border. In summer, sow foxglove and honesty to flower the next spring.

clear plastic bag

side stem or length of stem for a cutting

dip in hormone rooting powder

From cuttings Buddleia, honeysuckle, privet and ivy cuttings can be grown in pots in July and August, or put straight into the ground in November. Cuttings root better if the cut end is dipped in hormone rooting powder.

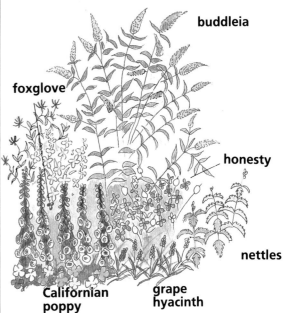

buddleia

foxglove

honesty

nettles

Californian poppy

grape hyacinth

BUTTERFLY OR MOTH?

Is it a butterfly or moth?
- Are the antennae feathery (moth) or club-shaped (butterfly)?
- When at rest are the wings horizontal (moth) or vertical (butterfly)?
- Is it flying at night (moth) or day (butterfly)?

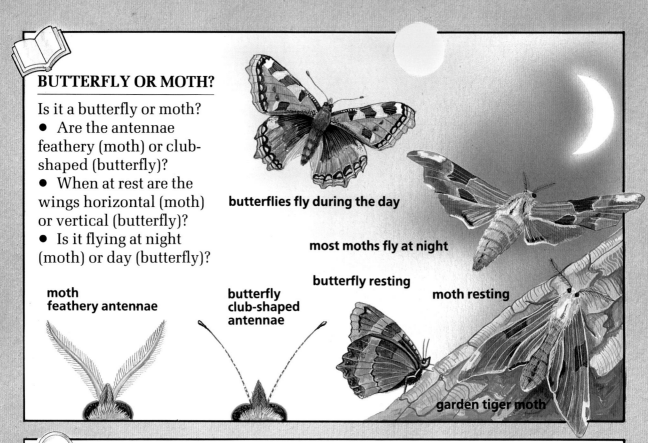

butterflies fly during the day

most moths fly at night

moth
feathery antennae

butterfly
club-shaped
antennae

butterfly resting

moth resting

garden tiger moth

ATTRACTING MOTHS

The nectar of various plants will attract moths, but try "sugaring" too. Add a mashed ripe banana and a tablespoon of beer or rum to a tin of black treacle, stir, and paint the mixture onto a fence or tree trunk on a warm, still evening. You can also set up various light traps. Ordinary bulbs can be used but mercury vapour bulbs, giving out ultra-violet light, are better.

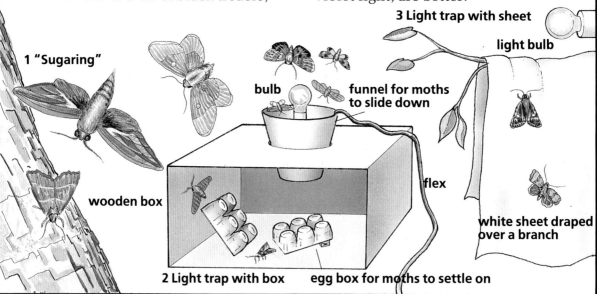

1 "Sugaring"

3 Light trap with sheet

light bulb

bulb

funnel for moths
to slide down

flex

wooden box

white sheet draped
over a branch

2 Light trap with box   **egg box for moths to settle on**

IDENTIFYING BUTTERFLIES

Only catch butterflies to identify them, then immediately let them go. Make a wire frame 30 centimetres across, then attach a bag of green or brown net (so insects can't see it coming). A nylon stocking will do. Make the bag at least 60 centimetres deep so the end can be flipped over the frame when the insect has been caught. This prevents it struggling and damaging itself.

DO NOT TOUCH

Butterflies are very fragile so do not handle them or keep them in containers for very long. The wings have very delicate scales.

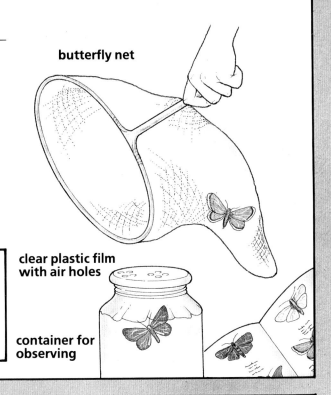

butterfly net

clear plastic film with air holes

container for observing

FOOD FOR CATERPILLARS

A nettle patch provides food for peacock, small tortoiseshell and red admiral caterpillars. It must be in a sunny spot and kept cut so there is a constant supply of young shoots. Cabbage and nasturtium leaves feed large and small white caterpillars. Honesty leaves feed caterpillars of the orange tip butterfly.

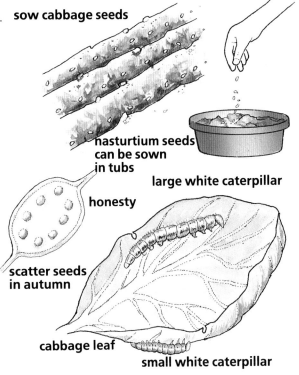

sow cabbage seeds

nasturtium seeds can be sown in tubs

large white caterpillar

honesty

scatter seeds in autumn

cabbage leaf

small white caterpillar

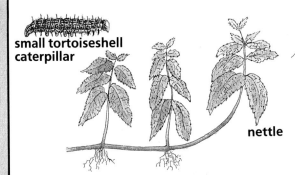

small tortoiseshell caterpillar

nettle

REARING CATERPILLARS

Before keeping caterpillars make sure you have plenty of their natural food. Look for them under leaves of trees and shrubs or tap the branches (see page 12). Search the tops of nettles for tortoiseshell caterpillars feeding under a web. If you handle them use a paintbrush. Only keep a few in one container with fresh food. Clean them out daily. Don't put nettle stems in water as they will rot. Remember that for pupation butterflies require twigs, moths need leaves or soil. As soon as the adults emerge and their wings have expanded and hardened, release them.

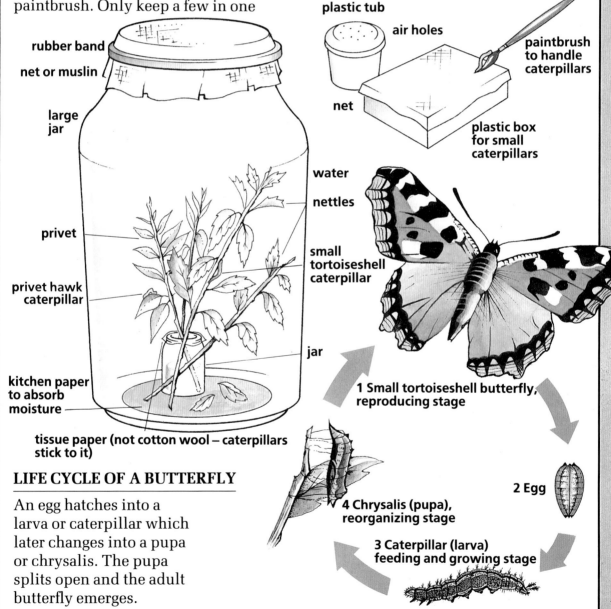

rubber band

net or muslin

large jar

privet

privet hawk caterpillar

kitchen paper to absorb moisture

tissue paper (not cotton wool – caterpillars stick to it)

plastic tub

air holes

paintbrush to handle caterpillars

net

plastic box for small caterpillars

water

nettles

small tortoiseshell caterpillar

jar

1 Small tortoiseshell butterfly, reproducing stage

2 Egg

4 Chrysalis (pupa), reorganizing stage

3 Caterpillar (larva) feeding and growing stage

LIFE CYCLE OF A BUTTERFLY

An egg hatches into a larva or caterpillar which later changes into a pupa or chrysalis. The pupa splits open and the adult butterfly emerges.

HAVE YOU SPOTTED?

Look out for these butterflies and moths. Keep a diary of those you see.

white plume moth

brimstone butterfly

yellow underwing moth

heart and dart moth

orange tip butterfly

underside of orange tip butterfly

holly blue butterfly

comma butterfly

wall brown butterfly

dot moth

small copper butterfly

silver Y moth

red admiral butterfly

large white or cabbage white butterfly

poplar hawk moth

common blue butterfly

painted lady butterfly

peacock butterfly

yellow shell moth

ENCOURAGING ANIMALS

Woodland and hedgerows are the natural habitat of many animals, and their destruction has meant less natural food and fewer nesting sites. In winter a bird table can save the lives of many small birds. Some birds would choose a hole in a tree as a nest site, but will use nest boxes instead. Bats, hedgehogs and insects can also be helped.

FOOD PLANTS FOR BIRDS

Grow a selection of berry-bearing plants like hawthorn, holly, honeysuckle and ivy for thrushes, blackbirds, finches, and so on. Finches also like teazels, sunflowers and honesty.

MIGRATION

Every year millions of birds fly from one part of the world to another to avoid bad weather and find food; this journey is a migration.

Marrow bones hung up or suet placed on a bird table will attract greater spotted woodpeckers, nuthatches and long tailed tits.

tree creeper

A variety of feeders, strings of peanuts and marrow bones can be hung from the table.

bird table

blue tit

Fit upturned flower pots or plastic drainpipe round the post to keep squirrels off.

Dunnocks (hedge sparrows) feed on seed.

Redwings and fieldfares migrate between Scandinavia and the British Isles (purple arrow).

Swallows migrate between Europe and South Africa (yellow arrow).

Arctic terns migrate between the Arctic and the Antarctic, a 40,000 km round trip (red arrow).

Song thrushes feeds on apples.

Starlings probe the lawn

Site bird boxes at least 2 metres off the ground, NOT on a hot south facing wall.

greenfinch

jay

Bat boxes fixed high up in trees may encourage bats to roost in them.

bat

collared dove

Vole feeding on grass seeds.

A dustbin lid supported by stones, makes an ideal birdbath.

blackbird feeding on worms from the lawn

Hedgehogs enjoy bread and milk, but dog or cat food is much better for them.

MAKING A BIRD OR SQUIRREL TABLE

WHAT YOU NEED

1.6 m post

wood

hammer

nails

40×40 cm

4 strips of wood, 36×2×2 cm

Where to put it Safe from cats, not too far from cover as some birds are uneasy in the open; near a window so you can see it from the house.

How to make it

1 Ask an adult to help. Shape the end of the post into a point.
2 Fix strips of wood to the flat wood with glue and nails.
3 Drive it into the ground and attach the top with nails.

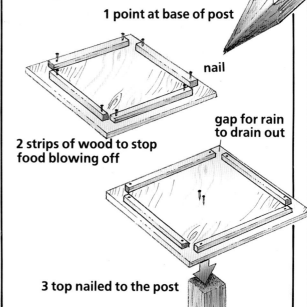

1 point at base of post

nail

2 strips of wood to stop food blowing off

gap for rain to drain out

3 top nailed to the post

FEEDING THE BIRDS

When to feed From October to April, and once you start you must continue. Stop in April when birds have young.
Feeding times First thing in the morning and in the early afternoon.
What to feed Finches are seed eaters so give ready mixed seed; marrow bones and suet for greater spotted woodpeckers, nuthatches and long tailed tits; peanuts, grated cheese, cooked rice and potato, moist crumbled bread, raisins, oatmeal, chopped bacon rind, uncooked pastry and cake. Avoid salted peanuts, salty bacon, desiccated (dried) coconut.

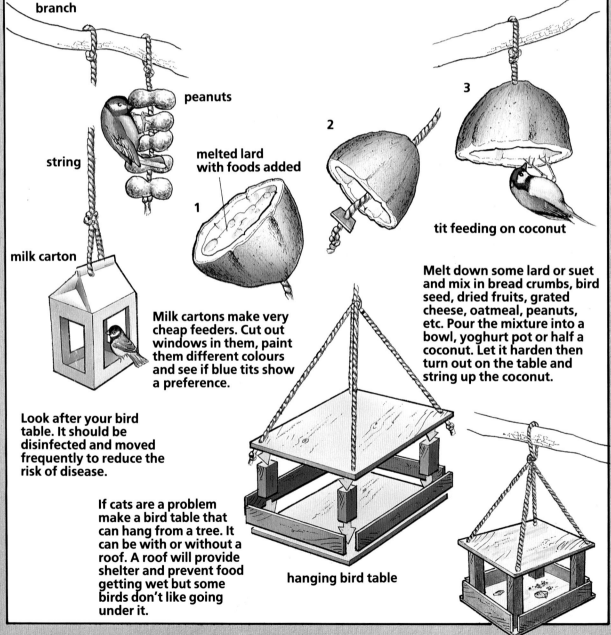

branch

peanuts

string

melted lard with foods added

1

2

3

tit feeding on coconut

milk carton

Milk cartons make very cheap feeders. Cut out windows in them, paint them different colours and see if blue tits show a preference.

Melt down some lard or suet and mix in bread crumbs, bird seed, dried fruits, grated cheese, oatmeal, peanuts, etc. Pour the mixture into a bowl, yoghurt pot or half a coconut. Let it harden then turn out on the table and string up the coconut.

Look after your bird table. It should be disinfected and moved frequently to reduce the risk of disease.

If cats are a problem make a bird table that can hang from a tree. It can be with or without a roof. A roof will provide shelter and prevent food getting wet but some birds don't like going under it.

hanging bird table

HAVE YOU SPOTTED?

Tawny owls may visit your nature reserve at night; listen for their alarm call *keewick*, or you may hear the familiar *toowhit-toowhoo*.

wagtail

tree sparrow

nuthatch

coal tit

blackcap

blackbird

redwing

marsh tit

robin

tawny owl

great tit

LET'S INVESTIGATE

What is the favourite food on your bird table? Put out 4 or 5 different foods. For 10 minutes, taking one species at a time, record what each bird collects.

bird \ food	seed	suet	peanuts	cheese
blue tit		✓✓	✓✓✓✓✓	✓
robin				

swallow
chaffinch
jay
thrush
greater spotted woodpecker

37

DID YOU KNOW?

Numbers of bats have dropped greatly; all bats and their roosts are now protected by law. Loss of habitats has meant fewer insects for them to eat. Also, many bats in lofts have been killed by chemicals used to treat woodworm.

BE A CONSERVATIONIST NOT A COLLECTOR

Remember, it is against the law to disturb nesting birds and collect eggs. Do not keep peering into nests as the parents may desert them.

SQUIRREL TABLE

Squirrels can be greedy and take all the peanuts from the bird table, but they can be fun to watch. Tie a peanut holder to a washing line, watch their attempts to get the nuts.

HEDGEHOG SHELTER

A pile of leaves or a hollow in the ground filled with dead leaves and covered with a piece of wood will make an ideal hedgehog shelter. If you are lucky one might even hibernate in it.

MAKING A BAT BOX

WHAT YOU NEED

A 45 cm E 11 cm B 21 cm D 20 cm C 20 cm C 25 cm

plank of wood 15 × 142 cm, sawn into 6 pieces

hinge

screws, nails or woodglue

How to make it

Use wood 2 centimetres thick so it gives some protection from outside temperature changes. Unplaned wood is best as the rough surface is easier for bats to cling to. Don't treat the wood with preservative – bats don't like the smell. Fix the box 3–5 metres up a tree trunk, facing south or west.

BIRD NESTING BOX

Nest boxes for blue and great tits should have an entrance hole 27 and 30 mm across respectively.

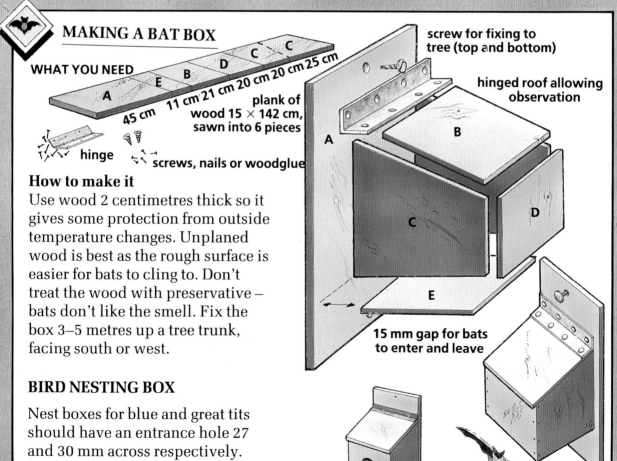

screw for fixing to tree (top and bottom)

hinged roof allowing observation

15 mm gap for bats to enter and leave

BUMBLE BEE HOME

In spring look out for large, furry bumble bees flying lazily over flowers in search of nectar. To make them a nest, bury a clay flower pot filled with dry hay in a bank of soil; leave the drainage hole showing or push a piece of tubing through it as shown here.

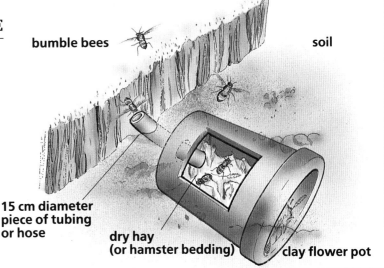

bumble bees

soil

15 cm diameter piece of tubing or hose

dry hay (or hamster bedding)

clay flower pot

UNDERGROUND HOMES

A sheet of corrugated iron left in long grass will shelter many animals. Ground beetles, centipedes, snails, slugs and millipedes soon move in, or maybe a slow worm or field vole. Slow worms are legless lizards; they are harmless and feed on earthworms and slugs.

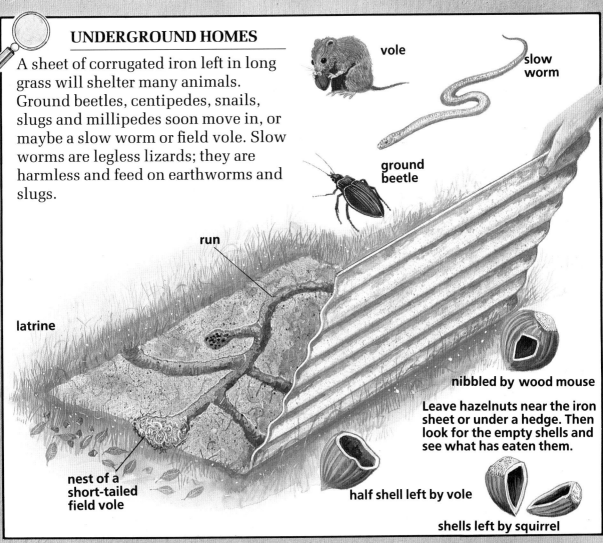

vole

slow worm

ground beetle

run

latrine

nest of a short-tailed field vole

nibbled by wood mouse

Leave hazelnuts near the iron sheet or under a hedge. Then look for the empty shells and see what has eaten them.

half shell left by vole

shells left by squirrel

MAKING A PATIO NATURE RESERVE

Create your own nature reserve in a backyard or on a patio. Make a pond in a barrel, set up mini habitats in tubs, window boxes and bottles. Tubs needn't be expensive – large flower pots, chimney pots and even buckets with holes will do. Use them to grow meadows, cornfield patches and plants to attract insects or their caterpillars. Wall flowers, honesty, tobacco plants, red valerian, Californian poppy, lavender, thyme, nasturtiums and nettles are all possible with the right soil.

cornfield patch

mini pond

meadow

bottle garden

herb garden

A MINI POND IN A TUB

If you haven't room for a pond, buy a half barrel, wash it out, then fill it with water; this makes the wood swell, seals it, and stops it from leaking. Empty it, and if necessary, line it with polythene. Put 8 centimetres of gravel in the bottom, then fill with water from a hose. Add some stones, then leave for 48 hours before planting. Note that a mini pond is unsuitable for tadpoles.

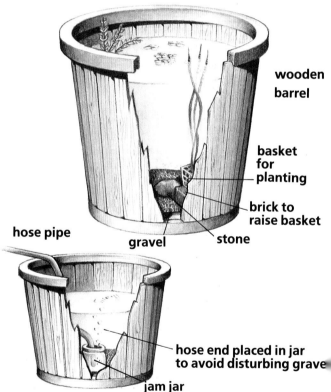

selection of plants

wooden barrel

basket for planting

brick to raise basket

hose pipe

gravel

stone

hose end placed in jar to avoid disturbing grave

jam jar

STOCKING YOUR MINI POND

Only add a few plants and keep them in baskets or pots. Watermint, water forget-me-not flowering rush and water milfoil are all suitable. Add snails and mud and your pond will come alive.

A BOTTLE GARDEN

Excellent for growing
flowerless plants, such as
mosses, liverworts and
ferns, all of which need
damp conditions. Glass
sweet jars make good
bottle gardens and are
easy to obtain. Add
gravel, charcoal, then
potting compost, with a
paper funnel if
necessary. Dampen the
compost, add some bark,
collect some mosses and
ferns and press them into
the compost with two
sticks. Put a cork in or
screw the lid on, but
loosen it if there is too
much condensation.
Liverworts are often seen
growing round the base
of house plants in garden
centres – ask if you can
have a piece.

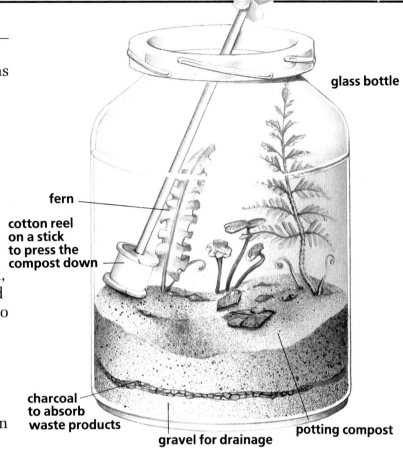

glass bottle

fern

cotton reel
on a stick
to press the
compost down

charcoal
to absorb
waste products

gravel for drainage

potting compost

A HERB GARDEN

Herbs and garden plants: sow seeds or
put individual plants into potting
compost. They may need liquid
fertiliser during the summer.

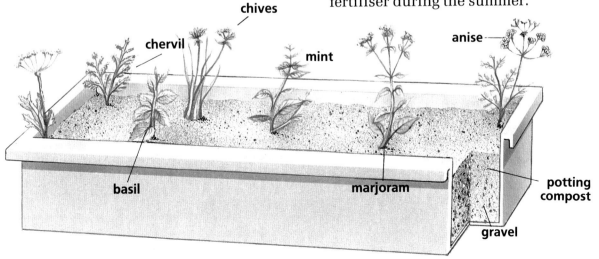

chives

chervil

mint

anise

basil

marjoram

potting
compost

gravel

USEFUL ADDRESSES AND FURTHER INFORMATION

Conservation organizations

British Butterfly Conservation Society,
Tudor House, Quorn, Loughborough,
Leics LE12 8AD.

Friends of the Earth (FOE),
26–28 Underwood Street, London
N1 7JQ.

Greenpeace,
30–31 Islington Green, London
N1 8XE.

Royal Society for Nature Conservation (RSNC),
The Green, Nettleham, Lincoln
LN2 2NR.

Royal Society for the Protection of Birds (RSPB),
The Lodge, Sandy, Beds SG19 2DL.
(The junior branch of the RSPB, **Young Ornithologists Club (YOC)**, is also at this address.)

St Tiggywinkles,
The Wildlife Hospital Trust,
1 Pemberton Close, Aylesbury, Bucks
HP21 7NY.

WATCH
(Junior section of the RSNC and its associated County Wildlife Trusts)
The Green, Witham Park, Lincoln
LN5 7JR.

World Wide Fund for Nature (WWF),
Panda House, Weyside Park,
Godalming, Surrey GU7 1WR.

If you are interested in any of these organizations, write, enclosing a stamped, self-addressed envelope, asking for details of membership and any information sheets, packs, etc. which they produce and which may be of interest to you. Several of the organizations have local groups that you can join and your local library should have the details.

Suppliers of native wildflower seed and plants

Many garden centres and nurseries now stock native wildflower seeds and plants, and native trees and shrubs. If you have difficulty in obtaining certain seeds or plants, try contacting the following suppliers:

John Chambers,
15 Westleigh Road, Barton Seagrave,
Kettering, **Northants** NN15 5AJ.

Emorsgate Seeds,
Middle Cottage, Emorsgate, Terrington
St Clement, Kings Lynn, **Norfolk**
PE34 4NT.

Hillier and Sons,
Winchester, **Hampshire**.

W. W. Johnson and Sons Ltd,
Boston, **Lincs** PE21 8AD.

Kingsfield Tree Nursery,
Broadenham Lane, Winsham, Chard,
Somerset.

Landlife Wild Flowers Ltd,
The Old Police Station, Lark Lane,
Liverpool L17 8UU.

Suffolk Herbs,
Sawyers Farm, Little Cornard,
Sudbury, **Suffolk** CO10 0NY.

Suppliers of pond liners
Your local garden or aquatic centre will
stock liners of various types and sizes,
but do shop around. Butyl liners,
which are guaranteed for 15 or more
years, can be bought "off the roll", and
can work out much cheaper than
packaged PVC or polythene liners
which have a much shorter lifespan.

Buying peanuts
It has been discovered that some
peanuts sold as wild bird food
contained high levels of aflatoxin, a
poison produced by a fungus which
can develop on peanuts. It can have a
serious effect on the health of birds and
if eaten in sufficient quantities can kill
them.

Make sure you buy "Safe Nuts",
approved by the Birdfood Standards
Association (BSA). If you have
difficulty in finding a "Safe Nut"
supplier contact:
BSA,
The Watermill, Mill Road, Water Eaton,
Milton Keynes, Bucks MK2 2UZ.

Squirrel food
Give squirrels natural food as far as
possible. Hazelnuts and sweet
chestnuts are favourites (if expensive),
and they also take whole maize and
wheat. Feed them only 3 or 4 times
a week so they do not become too
dependent on it. Don't give them too
many peanuts; the growth of young
squirrels can be seriously affected if
they rely too much on peanuts as their
main source of food. Squirrel food can
be obtained from:
Duffetts of Ryde,
Corn Merchants, High Street, Ryde, Isle
of Wight.

GLOSSARY

Alga/algae a simple green plant found in ponds.

Antenna/antennae a "feeler" of an animal like an insect, for smelling and touch.

Aquatic plant or animal that lives partly or wholly in water.

Arthropods animals with a hard outer skeleton and jointed legs.

Bacterium/bacteria tiny organisms, each made up of one cell. Some help in decomposition.

Carnivore an animal that eats meat.

Caterpillar the larva of a butterfly or moth.

Centipedes long, flat-bodied animals with one pair of legs on each segment or section of the body.

Chrysalis the pupa of a butterfly or moth.

Community all the plants and animals living together in a habitat.

Decomposition the breakdown of dead animals and plants, mainly by bacteria and fungi, with the release of nutrients into the soil.

Ecology the study of living organisms, their relationship to one another, and to their environment.

Ecosystem the environment of a particular habitat.

Energy a basic need of life. All energy comes originally from the sun.

Environment everything surrounding an animal or plant, including the atmosphere, climate, type of soil, and other animals and plants.

Fertilization the joining together of a male and female sex cell; in flowers this produces seeds.

Fertilizer a substance, like a chemical or manure, that enriches the soil.

Fertility the level of plant nutrients in the soil.

Food chain a feeding relationship; starts with a plant and forms links through which energy is passed.

Food web a set of interlinked food chains in an ecosystem.

Fungus/fungi a plant-like organism made up of branching threads. They play a vital part in decomposition.

Harvestmen animals with 8 legs, often mistaken for spiders. They have one part to their bodies and the second pair of legs is the longest.

Herbivore an animal that eats plants.

Hibernation a resting period during cold weather.

Insect an animal with three parts to its body, three pairs of legs, one pair of antennae and sometimes two pairs of wings.

Invertebrates animals without backbones inside their bodies.

Larva/larvae the first (feeding and growing) stage in an insect's life.

Leaf mould a crumbly mixture of partly decomposed dead leaves.

Migration movement of animals from one place to another according to the season, to escape bad weather and find new food supplies.

Millipede long, thin animals with many body sections or segments, each of which has two pairs of legs.

Mineral a simple chemical that a plant needs in order to grow.

Moulting occurs when insects, and arthropods, shed their hard, outer skeleton, and replace it with a larger one which has developed underneath.

Native an animal or plant which lives wild in an area and has not been brought in by man. Native trees support a much greater variety of wildlife than those introduced to an area.

Nectar a sugary liquid produced by flowers to attract insects.

Nutrient a chemical substance that a plant or animal needs in order to grow.

Nymph the young stage of certain insects, e.g. dragonfly and mayfly.

Omnivore an animal that eats both plants and animals, e.g. humans.

Organic anything which was or is, or part of, an animal or plant.

Organism an animal or plant.

Ovule contains the female sex cell of a flower.

Pollen a yellow dust produced by the anthers of a flower and containing the male sex cell.

Pollination occurs when pollen grains are transferred from the anthers of a flower to the stigma of the same or another flower of the same type.

Predator an animal that kills and feeds on another animal (the prey).

Pupa/pupae a stage in the life cycle of some insects, when the adult develops.

Seed is produced from an ovule after fertilization.

Seedling young plant grown from seed.

Species set of animals or plants that look similar and breed successfully.

Spiders have 8 legs and a body made up of two parts; they make silk.

Stamen the male part of a flower.

Stigma "catches" pollen.

INDEX